ATTORNEYS:
The Art of Public Speaking

"All the world's a stage…"

Carolyn Franklin M. A.

voicedynamicscf@yahoo.com

All Rights Reserved 2018

ISBN-13:978-1729826737
ISBN-10:1729826733

No Duplication Without Written Permission

Contents

ATTORNEYS: The Art of Public Speaking 1
KNOW YOUR AUDIENCE 4
RHETORIC (REH toh rik), "THE ART OF SPEAKING, ... 6
THE HISTORY OF RHETORIC 10
    The "Three Proofs of Aristotle" 10
THE THREE PROOFS OF ARISTOTLE 12
    ETHOS 12
    LOGOS 15
    PATHOS 15
THE POWER OF ATTITUDE 20
TO ADDRESS THE COURT 22
    STAGE CENTER 25
    ACTING "BUSINESS" - Distractions 25
    STATE YOUR NAME WITH CONFIDENCE 26
    STAGE FRIGHT PROBLEMS ARE COMMON BUT
    NOT FATAL 28
    EASING SYMPTOMS OF STAGE FRIGHT 32
    DISTRACTIONS 36
    OUTLINES 37
    EYE CONTACT 39
    LIES AND LYING LIARS 39

SMILES	42
MNEMONICS ("ne MAWN ics")	45
"SET UP" YOUR AUDIENCE	45
VISUAL AIDES: Hold them <u>STILL</u>	47
VIDEOS (MIRRORS)	47
AIR CONDITIONING	48
YOUR VOICE – HOW YOU SOUND TO OTHERS	49
LOW vs HIGH PITCHED VOICE	50
YOU SHOULD DROP YOUR VOICE AT THE END OF A SENTENCE	51
UP-SPEAK and GROWL	54
INTRODUCE A NEW IDEA - SPEAK SLO-O-WLY	56
ABOUT THE AUTHOR	62
OTHER BOOK BY CAROLYN FRANKLIN	63

ATTORNEYS: The Art of Public Speaking

As an attorney you're an actor, stage center, the lead role in a life drama. And, now, in court, the moment you dread, you step into the spotlight – you're on! Your mouth is dry, sweaty hands - memory blanks out - your feet won't move ...stage fright hits hard.

You've spent years at Prestigious U in Massachusetts, got your J.D., Magna com laude - all the gold seals and parched paper accolades available; you graduate, and then, realize you should have majored in drama. You find appearing before a judge, a court, a jury, requires skills foreign to you - acting! Drama. Parsing. Thinking on your feet! Verbal dancing, rhetorical dueling.

As the old song from the '40's, "It ain't whot'cha do hit's the way whot'cha do it."

Yes, indisputably! When you're arguing or presenting a case, it's not so much *what* you say, as *how* you say it that's the key to success. (I tried to research the song, but it's long gone.)

This is normal. Most people are not born performers. As an attorney your role requires you to appear calm, in control in the spot light, stage center – but, what if you make a mistake....? How can you look good?

Here's how:

Learn the strategies of actors who live through "stage fright" – use their method that convinces you to believe them in their pretense - their act. As an attorney your role is to seem calm, trustworthy, in control – your clients must believe in you.

Stage fright techniques to manage:

>   shaky voice
>
>   gestures
>
>   breathing
>
>   sweating
>
>   blank mind
>
>   dry throat
>
>   bathroom needs
>
>   handle distractions

Subtle, physical, strategies include:

>   eye contact
>
>   voice inflection (influence the court, frustrate the opposition)
>
>   pauses
>
>   stance…posture ("posturing")

The issue of gender, male and female attorneys, needs to be addressed. The public doesn't see you as "attorneys" – they see males and females – the *role is the same, but the acting - the <u>delivery</u> - is different.*

(Let me address the word "posturing." In my speech class a student mentioned that her gym instructor was teaching them "posturing." I was appalled. I explained that "posturing" meant to act as a phony, pretend to be someone you're not - *don't do posturing*! This is not an isolated incident of gym teachers attempting to join academia - they should not be allowed to talk, only blow a whistle.)

There are "tricks" only a man can use effectively to influence the court and, at times, female attorneys have impressive leverage. Use all the advantages you can!

KNOW YOUR AUDIENCE

One critical adage in Public Speaking is: ***Know your audience!***

Who are they? Where are they from? Blue collar, CEO's, housewives, McDonald's best burger makers, Ph. D's, engineers, or, Yeah man, if it feels good just do it…?

How can you "talk" to someone, if you don't know who they are?

I've been there; I've done it - as an opera singer. You think presenting a case is hard? Try hitting a high C in front of a thousand critics and know you'll die if you miss! Everything in this book - control nerves for a stellar performance – works!

Yes, "all the world's a stage" and, as an attorney, you're stage center in court – all eyes are on you. The spot light blinds you – your mouth goes dry, your hands are wet and you have to go to the bathroom – NOW!

An attorney "acts" a certain role, *persuades* people to believe that he or she will bring the case to a happy ending where you all line up stage center and take your bows to wild applause.

"…we strut our hour… to be seen no more." No one constructs an idea the way Shakespeare does; he is a master of words, innuendo and insinuation – much like an attorney – ask Portia. A presentation for court is crafted, mastery of words is critical, but words alone can be dry bones – rhetoric is the muscle.

This "persuasion" - "muscle." is called "rhetoric" and was invented by Aristotle, who, like Shakespeare was a master of concepts, words and mind manipulation.

KNOW YOUR AUDIENCE

Rhetoric is incorrectly defined as "the art of speaking" – it is not. It is "the art of *persuasion*" - the totality of : the environment, the occasion, the case at hand and the personality of the lawyers –the actors - and, most important, the audience.

This book explains the "everything else" - the "no words" part of acting. How and why you, in your role in the courtroom, can prepare ahead of time to control and understand personal annoyances such as: sweating, dry mouth, forget your words, shaky voice and a general fear of failure.

It's easier than you think.

RHETORIC (REH toh rik), "THE ART OF SPEAKING,

However...the "art of *speaking*" is absolutely meaningless.

In Communications, you will learn there are many ways to communicate, only one of which is "speaking" - using audible words. There are *many ways with out words to communicate,* and they're the ones that speak the loudest.

According to Albert Mehrabian, there are two ways to "speak:"

1. Verbal. Where you use words Relying on words to communicate is dangerous and sketchy. As attorneys you're no doubt aware how many times someone says, "But, I didn't mean that - what I meant was…"

2. Non-verbal. Here you use no words; you communicate by "body language." Mehrabian says words are roughly 3 - 7% verbal, so that leaves 93 - 97% non verbal. The term "body" language is deceptively misleading. Included in "non verbal" language is:

The kind of car you drive:

is it clean?

do the brakes work?

is it paid for or leased?

can you parallel park?

RHETORIC (REH toh rik), "THE ART OF SPEAKING,

does it have a stick shift?

The kind of job you have:

how much money do you make?

are you hourly, salaried, self employed?

what's your title, "hey you," Doctor,

Barbie, Mr.?

The house you live in:

5 bdrms, 3 1/2 bths?

do you have a gardener?

back yard covered in weeds, old tires?

second mortgage?

high-end ZIP?

Your general behavior:

are you early to meetings?

do you keep your promises?

do you live on credit, pay back loans - promptly?

yawn with your mouth open in public?

say "please," and "thank you?"

Do you have a pet:

chained in the back yard?

sleeps with you?

thoroughbred, stray, attack dog?

fed choice dog food, scraps, overweight?

Your level of education:

do you say, "Him and me went…"?

use French phrases?

read real books?

know how to spell vicissitudes?

you can pronounce "Proust" correctly?

That list is a small part of non-verbal language that people subconsciously note and use to assess your value in relationship to them. Today it's fashionable for someone to say, "I don't judge people."

Utter nonsense!

RHETORIC (REH toh rik), "THE ART OF SPEAKING,

We judge people all day in every way, we don't admit it to ourselves; but as social beings our likes and dislikes are standard, pervasive *human* behavior.

An accurate definition of "rhetoric" would be, "The art of persuasion." The main reason we communicate purposefully with others is to persuade them to do something for us. We want to be:

    liked

    believed

    appreciated

    taken seriously

    valued

It's all about "me."

THE HISTORY OF RHETORIC

Around the time of 5 BC, the Italians and Greeks, among others, were constantly at war. There was no "Greece" or "Italy" at that time, but rather a collection of cities which were also states; they were "city-states." Every city had its own king and army. After a war, if the king of the city-state were killed, there would be no one specific to inherit the kingdom, the vast estates or properties. People, relatives, neighbors, would get into a verbal "war" to try to determine ownership of the lands and businesses.

Usually there were no will or deeds to establish ownership of the estates; the people who argued the longest or strongest or, had the most compelling argument, won the case.

Also at that time there were men, mostly in Sicily, who studied the art of speaking and created clever ways to argue before a judge. They traveled around Europe, teaching how to prepare a case, settling disputes and demonstrating the power of a constructed speech. These men were called "sophists" (wise men).

Among these men were two who were prominent in Italy and Greece, Quintilian and Cicero. They further developed the art of speaking and were among the first to be called lawyers.

The "Three Proofs of Aristotle"

Aristotle was one of those incredible personalities who could separate himself from the surrounding conditions and observe interaction among people. He studied behavior and constructed labels that accurately described that behavior, the interaction, -

among groups, individuals, their probable motives and possible conclusions. Beyond genius!

Apparently he was Obsessive Compulsive, maybe even Attention Deficit Hyperactivity Disorder…he observed events, noted statements, catalogued thoughts, ideas and behavior as well as label abstract "things" as he ran across them.

Aristotle was an organizer; he listened to lectures and speeches and watched the process in action; he noted various categories of verbal manipulation in speeches and labeled them. To prove that a man was a good speaker, Aristotle created the specific characteristics of *Ethos, Logos and Pathos, to prove a person's credibility.*

These three characteristics of speeches, (*all* communication) are called:

THE THREE PROOFS OF ARISTOTLE

ETHOS

The FIRST AND MOST IMPORTANT of the proofs.

For his credibility, liking, trustworthiness and good character, a man demonstrated his skill as a persuader, speaker, by having specific strategies to strengthen the audience's belief in him. It's critical to be believed and trusted to create a following. Some means of establishing credibility are:

Is a person:

> Trustworthy
>
> Likable
>
> Ethical
>
> Charismatic
>
> Well-known
>
> Suitable social standing

If a person fits neatly into the above descriptions, that person will be singled out to be a leader in some capacity. However, in reality, someone could meet the above description and be reprehensible, such as Bernie Madoff.

As an attorney, it's imperative that you appear "ethical," trustworthy; you need ethos of the same standards and quality as doctors or priests.

Listed are some strategies appropriate to use in your presentations.

Transition: The word "trans" is a Latin word meaning, "across." It takes you from one point to the next. It's imperative that you keep your audience with you at all times, so if you plan to change the subject, you must "tell" your audience what you're going to do - use a transition: "I have been telling you about the robbery on 42nd Avenue, now *I'm going to change the subject* and say John was an altar boy at St. Anthony church."

Numbered transitions: "There are three reasons why you need…1. You should… 2. There is always a…, and 3. You can't…"

Verbal transitions: "And now, I'm going to change the subject. Let's look at why…"

FYI there are **silent transitions** also: Nod your head, shrug your shoulders, hand gestures that suggest helplessness, happiness, grief…

Keep your audience with you at all times.

Emblem: Today an emblem might be referred to as an "icon." It's a sign, picture or design that sends a specific message. A apple with a bite out of it represents an innovative corporation worth billions.

Red Herring: At times, if a question is best avoided, a person may use a red herring. This is to drag the hunter off scent and he loses his prey; it's a distraction.

Nancy Pelosi was questioning Condoleeza Rice; she asked "Condi," "Why did you lie to the American people about weapons of mass destruction?" "Condi" totally knocked Nancy off-target. "Are you impugning my integrity?" Nancy shut down, "dragged off course."

(When someone does a red herring on you, pause, look them directly in the eyes, don't smile, repeat your question word-for-word, then wait for an answer. If they still don't respond, keep repeating the process until you're satisfied - don't let anyone control you. Maintain eye contact.)

Enthymeme: This is a rhetorical syllogism. A syllogism makes sense: All dogs have tails, but not all tails have dogs. An enthymeme is a comparison, but a non-sequitur (usually done by women). "John has bad manners; he eats with his hands." "But he's good to his mother." (Note: It is characteristic of women to placate, excuse and ignore bad behavior in men. Usually, if a man's character is being attacked, a woman will step in to defend him no matter how disconnected the ideas are. They rarely defend women.)

Illustration: You make a "picture" with your hands or body. Someone says, "What does a banana look like?" You do your best to "draw" the shape of a banana with your hands - you "illustrate" it.

Or you might want to "illustrate" a sample of Irish dancing; stand up straight, put your arms down the sides of your body, kick up your heels and go tapping across the floor.)

Stories: Everybody loves stories:

Once upon a time, there was a robber who used a bow and arrow to threaten rich people. He wore a red pointy hat, a green vest and rode a white horse...

LOGOS

The **SECOND IMPORTANT** proof. Facts, *just facts,* accurate, current and verifiable. Logos can be:

> Statistics
>
> Charts, tables
>
> Wills
>
> Contracts
>
> Journal articles
>
> Eye witness
>
> Signed, dated documents
>
> Authorities, experts (doctor, lawyer, scientist, etc.)

The more facts you present to support your cause, the more trustworthy the speaker is. From this word we get: logic, logical, logistics.

FYI be careful who your eye witness is. A nun, priest or police officer is good. Your girl friend or your Mommy is questionable.

> *I had a friend, a priest, who was in a car accident, not his fault. As it happened a car load of nuns were witnesses. He won his case.*

PATHOS

The **THIRD IMPORTANT** proof. This is the most commonly used Proof and the most malleable. It's a ploy, a dramatic twist to win your case, or your cause. It's the proof where you make someone laugh or cry, feel sorry or happy for you - you need the "story" to win their confidence *at any cost*.

This Proof is the one where you tell the story, how hard it was, how you suffered - you "draw" your audience into your "story," your "drama," so they'll give you anything you want - you win. Not one bit of it needs to be accurate, although your "drama," your "story" should be based in truth.

And, if possible, your story should be one of perseverance and success; everyone loves a happy ending.

When you have no evidence you rely on emotion, opinion. This Proof requires no data, no facts, no witnesses - it's all opinion and emotion. From the concept of "pathos" we get the words: pathetic, pathological, pathogenic - all meaning death, dead or some heavy concept of great suffering.

> *There was a case on Judge Judy. A woman was suing her brother for a computer that had belonged to a brother who recently died of AIDs. She recounts his death, acting out all the death indicators. "He was dying of AIDs (cough, cough), I was holding his head in my arms (snivel, tears), I looked into his sweet face and he said, '(cough, cough, gasp) you (gasp) can have the computer.'" head falls down, he's dead. Her other brother, the defendant said, "No, he didn't." She lost the case in spite of her superb stand-up drama.*

People love stories; they like to be entertained; they'll listen more closely to your message. In general, if a speaker has a weak message, very little, or no, facts, he/she will use a great deal of pathos to move the audience to action. We've examined stories, anecdotes, emblems, red herrings and enthymemes. *Now, let's look at* some additional "pathetic" strategies. (That's a transition.)

Hyperbole: "over-the-top" stories or illustrations. Paul Bunyan and his ox "Babe" are prime examples. If something is big, make it BIGGER. If something hurts, howl in pain (that's an *illustration*). (This is a place where the voice comes in handy. You can talk louder, raspy, sweet, very high or low pitch, whine…all "special effects.")

Illustration: Again this is a free-choice demonstration of getting your point across. A dog bit your client. You "see" the dog coming, you cringe in fear, leap back in horror - the dog leaps up to your ankle and tears your flesh. You howl in pain…and win the case for thousands.

Loaded words: These words have built-in illustrations, pictures - very effective.

Four 18 year old male varsity athletes had consensual sex with an older prostitute. After they were done, they beat the woman, broke her nose, her ribs, a leg, and her eyeglasses. The woman reported the incident to the police; she broke the law as a prostitute - she didn't have "clean hands."

But, the District Attorney reasoned, when the attack took place, the "act" was done - at that point she was no longer prostituting - she was within the law. At trial each boy had a mommy, daddy and attorney.

The older woman had only the D.A.

*The defense attorney referred to his clients as: "These **boys, kids**, immature, didn't know what they were doing, **high school** boys…" The "boys" were smirking - done deal!*

The prosecuting attorney referred to his client as "This **lady,** *alone, hurt, attacked by those 4* **men**..." The 4 "men" got 30 years each. They stopped smirking.

In a "loaded" word, the drama, or picture, is built in. By calling 4 varsity football players "boys" you get a very different picture than 4 "men" - mature adults capable of rational behavior. In calling the older woman a "lady," the District Attorney substantially upgraded her social position.

Ad hominem: This is a negative, personal reference, usually done in election campaigns, but often it's done at your job; someone "bad mouths you" behind your back, lies about you or exaggerates a problem you may have.

Ridicule: Make fun of another person. This is not effective unless the person doing it is clever and understands the technique. You can only ridicule someone based on actual "truth." As Cyrano De Bergerac, you can only make fun of his exceptionally large nose - an outstanding opportunity for ridicule.

This strategy is cruel, hurtful and can backfire. It should be used only under dire circumstances. If you use this strategy you can lose your followers. If you want an excellent example of ridicule, read about Cyrano De Bergerac - really droll.

Parsing: you use a word exactly as it means, you don't assume or impute meaning.

Years ago in his 'Checkers" speech, Nixon was accused ofof "mis-handling" money from his campaign funds - $18,000.00. He swore he took none of that money for his "personal" use.

That was absolutely true. The word "person"-al means "for your person, on your body" - that would be toothpaste, shaving cream, hand lotion... "person"-al stuff. He didn't use any of that money on person-al stuff - he used it on yachts, sports cars, blondes - just kidding! but you get the point!

When Clinton was dilly dallying with Monica Lewinsky, he attended a luncheon at the "700 Club," an organization of thousands of Christians, where it's imprudent to lie. (This is a syllogism: "Christians don't lie; Clinton is a Christian so Clinton doesn't lie.") He was asked, "Is there anything going on between you and Monica Lewinsky?" He was very careful to parse, "No, there IS nothing going on between me and Monica." And, he was right - he "IS" facing hundreds of Baptists. But, maybe yesterday...? Tomorrow...?

THE POWER OF ATTITUDE

Your Attitude is a foundation of winning. It states, "I'm the one in control - the winner - I am!"

> *I don't wear a watch and occasionally I need to know the specific time. I was in Athens, in the huge air terminal on a marble stair case observing the passersby to see who I could ask the time. I saw an American businessman, walked down the steps to him and asked the time. He was startled. "How did you know I was an American?" I shrugged my shoulders, "You look American." To me, it was obvious. Then, years later in reflection, I thought, "Hmmm, how did I know he was an American?"*

It was *obvious;* we are one-of-a-kind. Americans stand out like a neon sign. He was well-groomed, tall, standing up straight, shoulders down, observing the passing scene. He had his overcoat slung across his arm and a briefcase loosely held in his right hand. He was totally in control; the irony is, people who are in "total" control, are unaware of it. They're used to being "top dog," confidence is ingrained in their attitude - they don't "have" attitude, they "are" attitude.

All around him were shorter people, slightly hunched over, looking down at the floor, eyes averted to avoid contact, walking rapidly. Every few seconds they seemed to glance over their shoulder or behind them as though to see someone after them. I sensed a feeling of paranoia.

The two attitudes sent vastly different messages.

Voice, sound and control, is a critical part of attitude; it's the Pathos, the strength, support and assurance of your professionalism; it's your ability as a person of trust and reliance. In short, the *sound* of the voice is a flexible and useful instrument in the manipulation and control of others.

Some people cringe at those words: "manipulation and control." But...it's what we do all day, every day – we just don't admit to it (out loud). In court (life), that's the name of the game – manipulation! And, like Superman, we use it for good.

The *sound* of the voice, *alone*, will carry your message...but...the voice is framed by several factors for added credibility, such as: your clothes, shoes, hairstyle, shave, beard, posture, eye contact, manicured nails, manners, accent... As an actor, you perform for the jury – they judge you - do you meet their expectations?

TO ADDRESS THE COURT

Posture The first thing an audience (jury) sees is your physical being: posture, walk (gait), height, weight and your outfit. Does this picture match the audience' expectations?

Who is the "audience" - a client, the jury, the judge? Are they educated, middle class, housewives, seniors, Republicans, Scout leaders…? Is the court in: NYC, Split Lip, Idaho, Los Angeles or Monongaheelachutah, MA? All very different people.

Your outfit must meet needs of the jury's expectations. As there are separate expectations between men and women's attire, let's look at the difference from the jury's view. Do you dress up, down, casual, stylish, conservative? Above all, be comfortable. Let's address dress:

> **MEN** are usually dressed well – except, two problems:
>
> 1. Successful men often carry their success up front, somewhat under their belt, but too far out front for your zipper. Please, keep your prosperity slimmed down so when your jacket is buttoned you look streamlined.
>
> 2. The pants are too long. The length should break just over the sides of your shoes - not drag in the back on the ground, nor pile up at your ankle. You may not be as tall as John Wayne, but you're perfect as you are. John Wayne was always hitting his head on a door jamb and had awful headaches – who needs that!

WOMEN have a problem – well several. We like to keep up with the current style, but that keeps changing. Short dresses, low cut front, skin tight, huge belts, slacks, dress, suit – oh, dear – what to wear?

To compound the problem, many women, even intelligent ones, feel style takes priority over fit and suitability. I *strongly* suggest otherwise. As a woman, ask yourself, what are you "selling"? Your intelligence? Your expertise as a lawyer? Your bosom? Or, your derrière?

"You" should be "out of the way" – unnoticed; your presentation, your logic, should be the star. Your clothes, hair and make-up should be subdued. You don't want the jury attending to your eye shadow; you want them to listen to your impeccable logic.

The "Red Carpet" in Hollywood seems to control the direction of style, either "controls" style or warps it. The "ladies" who pose on the Red Carpet appear to be locked in competition to show the most body parts, and BIG is apparently the criteria for the body parts.

Watching the Hollywood parade reminds me of a Monty Python production.

Potential "costume" problems for women:

> 1. Blouses should be tailored, maybe button up beyond the cleavage? Subdued colors. The buttons should close easily in front. One trick I learned, I sew up the front of the blouse thus avoiding "pop-out" problems- it's already obvious I'm a girl.
>
> 2. Jackets should be loose, fit well in the shoulders and waist. One glaring problem I've seen on ample-bosomed women, the jacket is buttoned so tightly at the waist I fear one day the button will fly off and impale a juror.

3. Unless you are 5'8", weigh under 125, *do not* wear anything that is form-fitting. Stay loose. Lumps and bumps are NOT attractive. Clothes that strain at the seams, put a strain on the jurors, too.

One of my close friends, an older Black gentleman, was faced with a major law suit. He hired a woman attorney, a blonde with long hair. She showed up at court for the hearing dressed in a red velvet slack suit. She lost the case.

I wasn't there, I don't know the particulars, but knowing rhetoric - non verbal communication, I can't help but think that, a Black man, showing up at court, with a hot blonde, dressed in a red velvet pants suit to represent him, was a poor idea.

You can stress all the "rights" you want, right to wear red velvet, right to be a blonde…but common sense has nothing to do with "rites". A better "message," a wiser choice, would be a woman, or man - of any race - not wearing a red velvet pant suit in court; the "costume" is not the star – your presentation is!

Jurors, clients, judges tend to focus on what's "wrong" and ignore what's important - it's human nature. I strongly suggest men and women who have a professional role, consult a tailor or designer to help create a suitable style for your body and professional image.

Eye contact is imperative. When you look directly into someone's eyes you send the message you're interested in what's being said - you care, you're listening. You have no idea how important this is to a woman. Women are so seldom "heard." In general men patronize us and move on. But when someone stops, looks and listens, we believe you help us and we trust you.

Teeth in America, are white and perfectly straight - at least they are in all the toothpaste ads. Cosmetic dentistry today is a miracle of ease and beauty and does make a difference in how the court perceives you.

Hair styles for women should be away from the face, away from the eyes. It's distracting and *annoying to w*atch while a woman continually reaches up to brush her hair from her eyes and face. *Eye contact is essential -* <u>*both eyes*</u> for ethos. We need to concentrate on what you're saying. If Henri l' Belle styled your hair, it's not an issue in the court. During time in court or with clients, a woman should *put her hair in one place and leave it there*.

STAGE CENTER

All of life, all social interaction, discourse, verbal and non verbal interaction is "show-biz" - entertainment on one level or another.

As Shakespeare notes:

"All the world's a stage and all the men and women merely players…"

Players – actors, assume many roles, many disguises. The roles lawyers play are expedient to the need at hand; one moment you're a comedian, or a priest, a stern father, tearful mendicant, an intellectual barrister or perhaps a serf.

Sometimes you have to think on your feet - there's no time to think in your head - that's "show biz," and the show must go on.

ACTING "BUSINESS" - Distractions

The term, "Business" in acting means purposeful "distractions," enhancements, ploys for attention that are artfully done to keep the focus where the actor chooses. This "business" is usually clever and subtle – to be obvious about distracting someone deliberately is not always in good form in front of an audience.

Sometimes it's referred to as "up staging," where a non-lead will momentarily take the spotlight off the lead onto himself.

It happens all the time on "Matlock," "Perry Mason," "Rumpole of the Old Bailey," and even the judge shows which I watch judiciously.

At a critical moment, someone will distract the drama by picking up a glass of water and taking a sip. They may drop something, cough, scratch themselves, yawn - they'll do whatever they can to distract the jurists or court from attending to the attorney "stage front."

It's human nature to follow a broad physical movement - hand, body, facial expression - it's instinctual, a survival atavism. If you need it, use it.

STATE YOUR NAME WITH CONFIDENCE

In transition Occasionally I give workshops for people "in transition," which translates as "people out of work." They've lost their jobs due to downsizing, takeover companies, etc. Since these people are older, seasoned, but less "techy," they need help finding a suitable job. I work with the voice, in particular, and also body language; when they apply for a job, what are they *really* telling the interviewer?

When it comes to stating your name, that is a dead-giveaway as to how you perceive yourself.

> *In one practice session of people applying for jobs, I ask the question, "What is your name, please?" The*

responses are very interesting and very revealing. I asked one woman, her name; she replied, "Mary xjhmmm." Her last name was deliberately obliterated. "What?" I asked. She repeated it the same way. I said, "You're recently divorced, right?" She nodded. "It was an acrimonious divorce, right?" She nodded. "You hate your ex-husband, right?" She nodded. "So why do you keep his last name? Why don't you use a name you like?" Instantly her attitude change. "Oh, no! It's a good name! I want the name!" "What is it?" She looked at me with pride and said, "Adam." I said, "Adam is a great name, good connotation, easy to spell and say. So, if you're going to keep it, why don't you say it with pride? You can love the name and forget the husband." Her whole attitude changed. She brightened up and said, "Mary ADAM," with great pride. When she did that, it was obvious she was proud of herself. This pride goes a long way in someone's perception of the speaker - it helps in getting hired for a good job.

Whatever your name is, the way you pronounce it states who you are. Unless you are not as famous as Clarence Darrow, put your head up, speak your name somewhat slowly, clearly and with sufficient volume. The way you say your name is the way you say "who" you are.

(As an aside, the only name I have ever heard that made me cringe is the name,

"Titsworth." How can a man go through life, the football team, his M.D., the installation as Grand PoohBah of the Golden Bikers, with a name so odd?)

Your opening lines One of the hardest challenges in Public Speaking is, how to start your speech. Once you get on the other side of the "opening," it's almost coasting from there.

I *strongly* suggest you avoid jokes - they don't translate. In our current diversity, humor from one country to the next doesn't travel well. Humor is further complicated by age; today's young people think what's funny is not always what a senior person would enjoy.

You can always laugh at yourself, I suppose - that is unless you're: disabled, a specific ethnicity, minority, disadvantaged, foreign born, or, from Texas.

In Public Speaking there are standard ways to open a talk:

> **Anecdote**: A short story relative to the point of the occasion.
>
> **Startling statistic**: Yes, as astounding as possible.
>
> **A quote:** Doesn't have to be clever, but it's better if it is.
>
> **A startling fact:** Gets their attention.
>
> **A joke:** You may want to get this cleared with someone before you tell it.
>
> **A compliment:** Firefighters have just put out the inferno in California. They deserve accolades.

STAGE FRIGHT PROBLEMS ARE COMMON BUT NOT FATAL

We no longer have "nerves," "butterflies" or "stage fright;" we use the impressive title, "speech apprehension" (we get paid by the syllable - like lawyers!).

Stage fright is a mis-direction of energy - we spend a mass of negative energy that *focuses on problems.* It's the opposite direction of where we want to go.

We focus on sweat, hands and knees shaking, dry mouth, will-I-forget-my lines, what if I drop something, make inappropriate sounds. We conjure up "Menehune", goblins - sitting at the bench or in the jury box, snickering at our ineptitude.

What a waste of energy!

Send *positive energy* on our delivery, our presentation. Do your best to feel good, optimistic. Every little bit helps.

When I was a kid someone showed me how to focus the sun's rays on a piece of paper by using a magnifying glass – the paper burst into flames! I was fascinated. Over the years I have learned how we burn ourselves – by *imagination* – far more powerful than the sun's rays - far more than reality!

We *imagine* catastrophe – a waste of energy! It's hardly likely the earth will open up and swallow us - anything short of that is certainly do-able!

Anxiety is so normal, almost everyone gets "butterflies" before a performance. And, oddly enough, it's a good idea. You want to be a little nervous, a little excited, apprehensive, as that keeps you "tuned" in to your audience.

But too much nervousness distracts from your "performance."

The following suggestions have been tried and work well in general. As long as you have a desire to move ahead and acknowledge "nerve" problems, over time *and practice* you will release much of the restrictions of nervousness - you may actually forget to be nervous! Being with an audience that wants to hear what you have to share can be interesting and fun.

Stress is here to stay and it's good in many ways. The only time it's bad, in fact, is when you let it take over your life. Stress helps keep you tuned up, alert, bright-eyed and bushy tailed. Without stress, tension and anticipation, a presentation can be flat, lack-luster and deadly boring – not good.

Unless you have a serious physical condition where stress is hazardous, avoid pills, fizzy drinks, uppers, downers … whatever. Stay with exercise, fresh air, fresh fruit, vegetables, fresh water, cut back on sugars, dairy, espresso, listen to classical music, read poetry.

There is no "cure," but, you can greatly reduce apprehension by:

Meditation But meditation is not a task you do "on the run." You actually have to sit down, relax consciously and breathe.

Imagery Every day, for 15 – 20 minutes, sit *alone, quiet.* Try the technique of "imagery" to prepare for important cases - it will help keep you calm, focused. Imagination is a powerful tool – it takes you from mind-thoughts to the "real" world – that which is "tangible".

To use "imagery" – *imagine* yourself in control, feel good, breathe calmly, handle papers deftly and surely. *Imagine* yourself seeing the jury - *feel the location, room, atmosphere…*, the judge is interested, positive toward your client's outcome. Always mentally picture - "image" - the scenes and feelings in the *here-and-now* – this is critical. If you imagine events happening in the future – that's where they will happen – in the *future*, and the future *never* materializes.

Breathe de-e-eply, slo-o-owly. Relax. Let go of all earthy problems, feelings. For the moment, you exist in another level of mind. For the moment, forget time, just breathe, (mouth closed) feel the breath going down to your diaphragm and then gently exhale. Do this as often as you can. The point is, to ***relax***.

Practice PRACTICE MAKES PERFECT! – OR, DOES IT?

Of course, you have to practice. Remember the old joke:

> *A cellist is lost in New York City. He stops a passerby and asks, "How do I get to Carnegie Hall?" Passerby says, "Practice man, practice!"*

But, sometimes you practice so much, the talk becomes stale – boring - you don't want to hear it again yourself! Take a breather when you need to; watch PBS.

BORRRING! When you get to the point where even you are bored with your presentation, the audience is too. Even though you smile, have eye contact – you're bored! The audience intuits boredom; there 's a slight monotone in the speech, a misconnection between the facial expression, eye-sparkle and vocal tones, - when the "music" in the speech is missing the audience drops out.

You need to think about what you're doing and perhaps re-new your ideas; take a course related to your vocation for possible updates. Everyone needs a change of pace every so often.

Get physical Put down all legal papers, take a brief walk in the fresh air, feed the ducks, run with your pet cheetah – clear your mind, get out of your head. Take deep breaths of fresh air – **get out of air-conditioning** – it's lethal to your system. Drink *water* – just *water*, stay away from sugar and milk products for awhile – and cut back on coffee!! – just for awhile.

Practice in the locale – so important. Go to the place where you're presenting. Walk around, feel the place, wear it, smell it – get comfortable. Where's the exit? Where's the bathroom? Where's the water fountain, cafeteria… Where does the sun hit in the afternoon from the window – in your eyes?

Is the room cold, too much air conditioning? Bring an extra sweater or jacket just in case. Too hot? Keep cold water handy. Drafty? Try not to get in the draft – not good for you.

Is the room dusty? Are you allergic to dust? Keep a tissue handy.

Hold any reading up, not directly in front of your face. The paper blocks your voice, cuts back on volume. Face your audience; don't turn your head this way and that way while reading, the sound will turn away from the audience.

Practice with dolls, magazine covers, the kids, neighbors, traveling salesmen…

Create a duplicate setting where you're presenting the case. Set up dining room chairs, put magazines with faces looking at you (I had my dolls and my opera- loving dog), pillows –simulate an audience - overcome "speech apprehension."

If you drop something do the obvious, deliberately bend over and pick it up. Take your time, talk to the court as you pick it up, if it's convenient. If not, still, take your time, be deliberate in your movements. Don't get flustered or hurry.

> *It was my first time to read the lesson at church. It seemed like a lot of words and I was worried it might be too long. Concerned, I asked the Deacon, "What if I need more time!?" He looked at me calmly and said, "Take it." A light went on - or course! Take it! I relaxed.*

EASING SYMPTOMS OF STAGE FRIGHT

Shaky, wet, and frozen hands are common. For sweaty, wet hands keep a small towel handy to wipe them, and also your brow if you need to. Be *deliberate* but casual. If you get flustered, so will the jury. Wipe your hands or brow *deliberately*. Use a small, neutral colored cloth as you focus on the witness. You might concentrate on the floor as though you had a revelation - people will follow your focus.

People automatically follow your eyes or your movements. So whatever you want others to see, you look at it, and so will they. It's instinctual.

The more you focus on the shaky hands, the more they'll shake.

Shaky knees As a young girl, in music training, convinced I would be a great opera singer, I sang at recitals, weddings, choir, etc. I was prepared with my selections, my hair was perfect and my dresses pretty.

But, in spite of this, my knees shook while I sang – I mean **SHOOK**! Annoying! Instead of listening, people would point to my knees and snicker! I despaired – what to do?

At this point it's necessary to explain for anyone who's not a singer, that, to hit a high C in front of an audience is to have an indestructible ego – second only to tenors! So, as a lyric soprano, I decided to rise above the knees and focus on the aria, mesmerizing my (adoring) audience into the magic of the music.

An odd thing happened…once I quit feeding the knees negative energy, they stopped shaking! I was elated! The "butterflies" never flew away, but they were manageable.

To put it in the vernacular, look at your shaking hands, dry mouth, urge to urinate – and say, "Forget it!" - you've got more important things to think about! The problem may dry up and fade away.

Sick to your stomach can be somewhat modified by eating "gentle" foods before a presentation, court appearance. Chicken soup is always a good choice, something light, not spicy.

However, it's best to see an M. D. or perhaps a nutritionist to ease your mind there's nothing more serious happening.

Dry throat is probably nerves. Keep water handy. Calmly, *deliberately*, pick up the glass or bottle and sip. If you're in the middle of discourse, take your time, people will wait. If you try to rush, you may make things worse.

And, should you accidentally slop water on your tie or blouse, be calm, take your time. *Calmly, deliberately*, mop it up. If you have presence of mind, you might want to make a little joke about it.

Avoid coffee, if possible; it's a desiccant, also avoid alcohol. Cool water is the best lubricant.

(For me, I find Hall's Eucalyptus cough drops to be a definite asset in keeping a throat moist. This is not an endorsement, but should anyone offer me money, I'll take it.)

Shaky voice This is probably due to lack of correct breathing techniques. It may help to relax and concentrate on deep breathing, but there, again, it's not as easy as it sounds. In short, the best remedy is to *relax* and do your best.

Mind blanks out is somewhat normal. Our mind moves at a rapid pace while the tongue and mouth plod along far behind. Sometimes our thinking races ahead of the words, then we lose our location in the speech - where am I! We panic!

What to do?

There are two actions you can take. One is:

> 1. Lie. Yes, lie. Pause, say something like, "Let me digress for a moment…" move yourself thoughtfully, deliberately - just a little. Look down at the floor as though Gabriel just sent a celestial message - speak slowly…(you might

even scratch your head or stroke your beard), then say, "…it is vital that the jury considers the inexperience of Geraldine, the accused…" Go on with some blather about Geraldine not having ballet lessons so she turned to robbing banks…you get the idea. It will buy a few seconds 'til you're back on track.

2. "Vamp 'til ready." In the music world when we lose our place we do a thing called, "Vamp 'til ready." The audience has no idea what we're doing and is comfortable. Take your time… you know, when the star is late, or his mind blanks out, he for gets the words, the chorus stands there, blank looks, then the pianist plays: "DA DA dumpty dumpty DA DA , DADA dumpty dumptyDA-DA– " until the star remembers who and what's going on – and then picks up where he left off!

Or, you could grab some detail re the case and bring it forefront to muse over vocally, seeming to have new insight into some trivia for the court to consider.

Bathroom needs Here, I can't help you. When possible try to make a trip to the bathroom before the presentation, otherwise wear Depends.

> In high school just before I sang for a program I'd always "have to go" a feeling of excruciating pressure resulting in various gymnastic poses in an attempt to relieve the discomfort. Victor, my piano accompanist, had frozen hands, In vain he would rub them, blow on them to defrost them, to no avail. We would be announced, and then walk out on stage looking like we didn't have a care in the world. We always did well.

DISTRACTIONS

Distractions– are a ploy in the theater, on stage, when one star want to disrupt another star's performance. It's dirty trick to confuse the person performing and take the accolades for one's self. But, it works.

The prosecuting attorney is expounding, or the defending attorney is about to make a key point, you can destroy their strategy by moving something such as your hands, head or body; move left or right, drop something, blow your nose, cough– it pulls the opposition off-track, distracts the witness or the court. To the person distracted, it's infuriating. It keeps the focus on you.

One distraction that is infuriating, yet seems "innocent" is the "quiet, late entry."

This is usually done by a woman. She will enter a meeting in process, 10, 15 minutes late. Everyone is seated. She'll look around as she comes in, smile apologetically to the assembly, pull out a chair - which bumps into neighboring person; she smiles and mouths an apology, set her gear down, then be seated, get comfortable and look at the people as though, "You may continue now."

Rest assured, this "late entry" has been rehearsed many times. It's a distraction to pull the leader off course. This is just one o many ruses that cover up interruptions to take away the focus on the leader.

The leader has two choices to react:

    1. Ignore the person, continue uninterrupted.

2. Stop the meeting, smile sweetly, ask Janine if she's all right, can we help you? Would you like some coffee? did you get a copy of the report - are you sure?

This is called sarcasm and is always a last resort.

Movement People follow movement. For attention, move something - an arm, a white tissue to mop your brow (or lime green scarf), drop the briefcase, sneeze , eyes and attention follow movement. Everyone will focus on you.

This is not "distraction," "movement" is to assist the court in understanding a specific behavior of some witness or event.

Gestures are "pictures" you can draw with your hands, face, eyes and body. You show how high the fence is by holding your hand up so far. Fear or joy can be registered on your face to enhance emotions of your client.

You should be somewhat judicial in your amount of pathos - your use of physical illustrations - don't confuse "gesture" with "jester" such as Johnnie Cochran in the O.J. Simpson trial.

"Sides" A "side" is when someone makes an "under the voice" comment. In the opera this is referred to as "sotto voce" - under the voice. Usually it's drollery or a sarcastic observation. These comments disturb the general flow of conversation or the point you're making. Just ignore them.

OUTLINES

Outlines – it's been mentioned to me that some attorneys are "boring." At times, we all are. Well, you can't all be Perry Mason or Ben Matlock (they have a script). **BUT** you can move things along smoother by using an outline.

When you present your case – the **facts** come first in order of importance; then the **"story"** fills out the background; you fill-in the padding, the pathos, around the facts. The outline is there to help you focus and have a smooth trip through the case. If you get lost, you can grab a thought from the outline and move on.

Decide your strategy for presentation; do you want the hard facts first, or do you want to slowly build up to the critical moment as a climax in the trial or case?

Have an outline with facts printed in **BOLD CAPS** in red ink and the supporting comments in green ink, other comments in other colors, maybe show the time-line in blue.

Place the references near the facts for sharper, speedier accuracy - information in an instant. This preparation is a non verbal statement of the acumen of the attorney. How sharp he or she is, how they have your case under control. You're in good hands - a positive non verbal statement.

Include in the outline:

>anecdotes

>comments,

>possible questions

>personal observances

Be prepared. It's tedious to wait while someone locates data from their watch pocket or the recesses of their brief case.

This type of organization might make your presentations more interesting, colorful and enjoyable for the court – and you.

COME PREPARED: NOTES, PENS, ERASERS, PENCILS, BLANK PAPER, WATER, TISSUE, SMALL CANDY BAR (NOT MELTABLE), DATA...

EYE CONTACT

Is critical. There's a general myth that if someone looks directly into your eyes when they talk to you, he or she is an honest person – no! Not so! A person looking directly into your eyes could be totally honest or an expert liar – there's no way to tell them apart - well, there is, but you need training in non verbal behavior.

For your credibility, have direct eye contact when you address a witness, a judge or jury. When you do this, people will assume you're honest, and trustworthy.

The jury will believe a witness who has direct eye contact even if that witness is deceptive. People tend to be very trusting.

LIES AND LYING LIARS

Social scientists have studied eye movements during, before and after someone is lying. Eye movements reflect liars; also body movements can betray falsehoods.

When you question someone, note any odd movements during their answers and examine them closely later to see if deception is evident. There are far too many body movements in lying to give at this point.

When it is likely a person is lying the eyes will:

> Go to the *right corner* of the eyes and probably look "up." The person seems to be looking "up" while he or she creates an answer. In studies it's been concluded the

right side of the brain is the "creative" side - therefore the "lying" side.

If eyes go to the left side they are probably truthfully recalling an incident. The left side is the "analytical" side. But nothing is absolute here.

As we noted with Bill Clinton, the eyes will blink on the specific word of the lie, such as "yes," or "no," "did not," or "Yes, I did."

"No (blink), I did not rob (blink) the bank." "Yes (blink) I paid back (blink) the money I owed."

Also a person lying may look up at the sky during deception, or lower their head and look at the ground.

Some people open their eyes wide when they lie, others narrow their eyes.

Recognizing a lie is a talent in itself. Some people recognize a lie by intuition; some people believe that certain types of people would never lie. Some people think most people are liars.

Scientists are narrowing in on some subconscious responses in liars. These responses are physical and subtle.

> *A young man I worked with was a pathological liar. Whatever you asked him, he would deny it - but, he would do a dance. Totally unconsciously his feet would start sliding around, back and forth. He was trying to "dance" out of whatever the problem was.*

As Judge Judy says you need a good memory if you lie.

TO ADDRESS THE COURT

You have to watch critically and with practice before you decide who's deceptive. It would be most unkind as well as expensive to accuse someone of being untruthful who is innocent.

Oh, yes, there are some very unscrupulous people who invoke the name of God while lying as though no one would call on God if they were being untruthful - even some politicians have done that!

Myself? I would be very hesitant to call on some all-powerful force to back me up in a lie - I'm afraid of lightening!

> *When Bill Clinton was at a "700 Club" meeting, the members there (mostly Fundamentalist Baptists) asked about his dalliance with Monica Lewinski and he replied with his famous parsing answer, "Nothing IS going going on," the "lie" monitor picked up a slight blink of his eyes on the word "is."*
>
> *The monitor records the readings on a graph and you can plainly see the jump in the needle on the words of the lie.*

Once you know what to look for, when someone lies to you, notice on the key word whether the eyes blink or not. If they blink - it's probably a fib.

> *I used to tell the girls in my class what to look for when a boy lied to them. Boys usually look directly into the girls' eyes and say, "Do you think...**I**...would lie...to **you**?" and then drop their head as though overcome with grief.*
>
> *The girls would scream with laughter because we've all seen it. It's a standard response by boys.*

SMILES

Smiles are as American as apple pie, hot dogs and baseball. We're expected to smile and suspected if we don't.

But, today smiles should be used judiciously; they can be misleading. The person smiling may think they're being friendly, open, but smiles may be interpreted differently. They may be interpreted as:

>friendship
>
>enticement
>
>amusement
>
>love
>
>calming
>
>agreement
>
>appreciation
>
>"thank you"

or as:

>ridicule
>
>fear
>
>hypocrite
>
>uncertainty
>
>confusion

overture to sex

As in all non verbal communication, what the "smiler" means and what the "smilee" reads may be planets apart. It's difficult to send the exact message intended. Much depends on the cultural expectations of both parties.

It's far more socially acceptable for women to smile than men - women are expected to smile – even attorneys. In some situations a woman's smile is an asset. For example:

As a woman attorney a smile sends the message:

> Smile reassuringly at the young women in the jury; you appear to them to be strong, capable and a great role model.
>
> Smile humbly to older women to acknowledge their wisdom and social standing (whatever it is).
>
> Be careful smiling at men – you can't be sure how they interpret it. If a man makes a joke, smile deferentially; appreciate the humor. Look alert and interested. Still, in this century, women are not always recognized for their intelligence and expertise - but, we persevere.
>
> When you introduce yourself, unless you're Elizabeth Rex, or, Helen of Troy, speak your name SL- O- W - LY, give people time to hearwhat it is.

SELF-CONFIDENCE - the Cowardly Lion in the "Wizard of Oz" had self-confidence all along - he just didn't have a certificate saying so. And, much of the time that's where our self-confidence is, on a piece of paper that says so.

The major problem with self-confidence is comparisons. We lack confidence because we tend to compare ourselves to others – so-o-o pointless! Maybe someone is smarter than you are. So what? Maybe someone is more successful than you are. So what! We're all good at something and not good at something else. We focus on the negative in our self but see strength in others.

You may envy someone for their perceived talents, they envy you for your strengths.

> *I was an ugly duckling in high school. Not acceptable for the "in" group. Some of the popular girls didn't like me. It hurt my feelings. Later on I became a tall swan and all the popular girls were short and dumpy. Now they liked me even less. But then I didn't get my feelings hurt - I didn't like them either.*

If your lack of self confidence is a problem, go to a good psychologist for a heart-to-heart talk. Meditate – develop the attitude you're thankful for all the talents you do have - keep a positive attitude for the talents of others. One day they may be your best friends and light up your life.

> *In college, in the Music Department, two very talented young ladies dominated performances.*
>
> *Tami was a beautiful, bubbly blonde while Arti was a dark haired beauty. Arti was by far more talented but Tami's bubbling got more attention.*
>
> *Arti confessed she was jealous of Tami's talent. I said, "Arti, Tami is a star, but you're the sun – she gets her light from you - her pale light makes you look all the greater."*

Yes, we shine off each other, we each have strengths and weaknesses – give thanks for your strengths and work on your weaknesses.

(I can't resist calling your attention to the ultimate example of lack of self confidence. Watch Rowan Atkinson in his "Mr. Bean" series. You can learn a lot from him.)

MNEMONICS ("ne MAWN ics")

Mnemonics is a Greek tongue twister meaning "memory". You set certain items in specific locations in the trial room or event location that will trigger your mind to recall key phrases and points.

For example:

> A clock might mean "time flies," "it's time for a change."

> A courtroom window might mean:
>
> "As we look into the future…"
>
> "What is our way out of this dilemma…"

> A red rose, "She's in the bloom of youth.."
>
> His Honor: "We must not be too quick to judge…"

"SET UP" YOUR AUDIENCE

To "set up" the audience is to alert them, get them ready for new information. Hold up the "lost will" so everyone can clearly see it. Then perhaps open with a "number" transition.

Say "**FIRST** I have new information that will completely reverse the court's decision in this matter."

Then, "**SECONDLY,** *I'll show you* how they applied various pieces of evidence."

Or, use a verbal transition:

"I am *going to tell you* about a current article on how to win every case and double your fee."

Then, slo-wly, deliberately, hold up the article, hold it still for a moment so *everyone* can observe it, then start talking about its relevance:

"This article, "W*inning cases and doubling fees.*" by Josh Enslee, CEO of Rational Goals….. (repeat the content of the article to be sure everyone heard it.)

This method gets attention immediately. You alert the audience you have critical information; give them time to absorb that. Then, present your data or visual.

People probably have their mind on "what'sfordinner," "Igottagetgas" in the car, my feet hurt…

"Setting them up" saves repetition, time, effort.

> *So often, while watching TV or listening to a lecture, I zone out. Then the speaker says, "…so this book is the exact one you need for that burning question about the origin of Life." Too late! I jump to attention and can never get the name of the book or author. As the "audience," I was not alerted ahead of time to get ready for new, exciting, **critical** information.*

VISUAL AIDES: Hold them <u>STILL</u>

<u>Visual aides</u> are often a book the presenter wrote, or a scientific treatise to be explained, so the speaker is already nervous or excited about the evidence he or she is exhibiting.

> *Often, when a speaker holds a book he wrote, he'll bounce it up and down to get your attention. You can't possibly concentrate on the title or the info if something is moving.*

Hold exhibits, visual aides, evidence, **UP,** *away from your face;* move them

S-L-L-O-O-W-W-L-L-Y

across the area; give the jury or audience a chance to focus, to comprehend the visual aid. Move the visual aid from side to side. Unless you need to point out some detail, say nothing – let the jury think.

Do not put evidence in front of your face - in particular, your mouth. The words get lost behind the object.

VIDEOS (MIRRORS)

<u>Videos</u> are a good way to trace your expressions. Rehearse in front of a video; if none is available, rehearse before a mirror. Do you see what you think the court sees when you emphasize the words, "My client is innocent!" ?

Speak the words as you record or while you look in the mirror. Practice various "readings", sad, happy, demanding, despair, choked up with emotion… You may look better than you think. But it's always a scare to see yourself from the outside.

AIR CONDITIONING

Air conditioning, in my experience is poison floating in the atmosphere. When I am in air conditioning for a period of time, I get a cold, bronchitis or the flu. I strongly suggest you spend as little time as possible indoors with the wonderful, comfortable air.

The same is true in airplanes. I get sick. If you don't, fine, but be aware if you develop chest problems, it may be due to the chemicals you're breathing in controlled atmospheres.

The best air to breathe, is, air. If possible stay at the beach or far up in the mountains. Get out of Dodge with all the fine dining and shops. It's better to breathe without coughing than blow your nose on cashmere.

YOUR VOICE – HOW YOU SOUND TO OTHERS

THE DELIVERY *IS* THE MESSAGE: The "message" to your audience, the judge, jury, opposing side, is in the delivery of the words, not necessarily the words themselves. Of course the words, per se, are critical, but *how they are delivered, how they are spoken,* is the actual message.

The sound of your voice and the way you say the words - the delivery, are far more critical than the words themselves.

KEY WORDS are like "music": They should be emphasized, differentiated in some way. Carefully read your evidence. Select "key" words to emphasize in some way. Sometimes the smallest word has the biggest meaning:

Speak each of these proud, indignant, shocked sounds:

"My client would *never* do that!"

"My client would never do *that*!"

"*My* client would never do that!"

Or:

Sad: "My client would **ne-**

ver do

that..."

AVOID THE WORDS: Really, like, so very, actually, basically.

They are like really, actually, basically so very, I mean like, so very immature. These words are almost exclusively used by girls up into their '30's. This is like actually so immature; it's a ploy to hang on to, like, crumbs of youth.

LOW vs HIGH PITCHED VOICE

A low-pitched voice is generally more interesting, more comforting, musical and trustworthy than a higher pitched voice. It's human nature. Often a higher pitched voice is sharp, strident and unpleasant.

Occasionally a woman will say to me about her voice, "My voice is so low - I sound like a man!"

In all my experience I met one woman who sounded like a man - like a truck driver who smokes cigars. This was on the phone. I about dropped my teeth when she said she was a woman!

It's *extremely rare* for a woman to sound like a man.

Voice in the stomach? There are people who have been told that their voice is in their stomach, or who have come to that vacuous decision on their own. So incredibly absurd.

The "voice" - the "strings" that make the sound, are actually in your throat in a box called the "larynx." As you exhale breathe, the "wind" (air) goes through the trachea, up through the voice box (larynx) and "moves" the vocal chords - the "strings," the same way the wind moves wind chimes. The "chimes" vibrate, make a sound. That's it - that's where the sound originates - **not in your stomach**.

You don't hear your real voice - everyone else does. People say, "My voice is too (whatever)," and, usually, they're far from accurate. If you're not sure of the pitch or sound of your voice, go to a classical musician – cellist - ask for an opinion on the sound of your voice, i.e. is it pleasant, trustworthy or does it need some adjusting. A cellist will tell you the truth.

Only, ever discuss voice, music, singing, professional talking, with a classical music teacher - **_classical_**.

YOU SHOULD DROP YOUR VOICE AT THE END OF A SENTENCE

Well actually, you don't "drop" your voice, you lower the pitch. This lower sound tells the listener you're done, it's final, your statement is secure, you know what you're doing:

> "And so, ladies and gentlemen of the jury, the facts speak for themselves – my client *is*
>
> **innocent."**

Lowering the pitch indicates finality, security and trust. Speak in the present tense; the future tense indicates something will happen – *in the future*. You don't want *future* results – you want them *now* – in the *present:*

> "And so, ladies and gentlemen of the jury, the facts speak for themselves – you *will* find my client
>
> **innocent."**

A weak conclusion – leave out the "will" –

> "My client **is**
>
> *innocent!"*

Monotone – some men think they speak in a monotone – not likely. But many men are culturally trained to speak predominantly in one pitch (a mono – tone). They believe pitch change takes on a feminine quality

No, not true - not at all.

To speak in a true monotone can be an indication of severe stress or a "tin ear" as musicians say, unable to distinguish pitches. To the listener, a monotone is

BORRRRING! The audience, shuts down, tunes you out.

The "music," variation of sound, attracts attention; speech is interesting, more meaningful.

If you think a monotone is a problem for you, go to a drama coach or *classical* singing teacher for guidance (or me!).

Vocal warm ups are vital to the voice, the body and the mind.

Here's an all-purpose voice exercise to do in the car, bathroom or in line at the grocer's:

> Stand, relax.
>
>> Relax your shoulder muscles, and your facial muscles; take an easy, de-e-ep breath.
>
> Be sure you're *relaxed.*
>
>> Then, Exhale gently *through your nose* and gently make the sound:
>>
>> mmoooooo , mmoooooo,
>
> do this through your nose as though you were a ghost.
>
>> Later, as you feel comfortable, add the consonants:

YOUR VOICE – HOW YOU SOUND TO OTHERS

looo loooo

wooo wooo

Then change the vowel to:

Moh… moh…

Hoh…hoh…hoh…

Loh…loh…loh…

The key is to relax and let the sound flooooow out of you - don't "work" at this.

Try to keep these sounds out of your throat – breathe them out of your nose carefully, let the sounds flow gently from your nose and sinuses to create a rich, pleasant, mature sound.

You want the sounds coming from your "nose" as that keeps your throat clear of strain, stress. You want your inner throat muscles to be as comfortable when you speak.

And NO, this is NOT a "nasal" sound. Forget you ever heard that word. "Nasal" means "nose" and, paradoxically the correct sound is when you don't use your nose!

Forget you ever heard that word.

This technique is called the "Belle Canto Method" and shapes a healthy, beautiful sound that will last you all your life. As a man, it will enhance your masculine qualities. As a woman it will make your voice more melodic, pleasant.

"Good sentences well pronounced" Portia "Merchant of Venice" Shakespeare.

UP-SPEAK and GROWL

Up-speak and Growl are current affections of women in their everyday speech patterns. The affectation is most unattractive.

It's fashionable for women to speak often in one of two styles: "up-speak," or "growl."

They're both *very unattractive* and, also, hard on your voice.

"Up-speak" is where phrases and endings of sentences go "up" in the middle of the phrase and at the end like a series of disjointed questions. . It's like riding over rough ocean waves.

> explain to you?
>
> evidence?
>
> trial?"
>
> "I'm going to
>
> some new
>
> that will change the

The "up-speak" affectation is *very immature.*

The "Growl" is spoken down in the center of the throat so the sound is raspy and obscure. It sounds like a farmer choking on his chewing tobacco.

Don't do it. It's very unattractive and hard on the throat and vocal chords.

People will hear to how *badly* you say something, not *what* you're saying.

(This is also a problem when someone has a strong foreign accent. People will hear the accent and not the words. As a doctor or attorney, you have a particular onus to speak clearly so clients can more easily understand you. If this may be a problem for you, get a speech coach. A teacher of classical music is excellent or a professional actor, dramatist, can better understand accents. ESL teachers are usually not good at correcting accents. They are amazing at teaching English, but not good, usually, at correcting the pronunciations. One ESL teacher I observed was training her students to say "Sunday" as "Snnnnn deee" there's no such word. It should be,

"Suuh…… nn deh eee"

the vowels are what we *hear*, not the consonants. The consonants make the word intelligent - both sounds are specifically pronounced - consonants and vowels.)

By the way "I can't help the way I talk, I can't help the way I sound - I was born with this," is SO not true! You can definitely change your voice if you put the effort into it. The voice is just a "tool" that can be adjusted with a little effort.

INTRODUCE A NEW IDEA - SPEAK SLO-O-WLY

There is a pervasive myth that to speak slowly is to insult the audience – this belief implies that the audience is dull-witted. I totally disagree - in both cases.

Engineers, in particular, those who think faster than can talk (*we all* do!) and feel if they slow down they'll insult their listeners.

And, partly, that's true. It's agonizing to wait for someone to finish talking when you know what the ending is. It's a struggle to be courteous and let them bumble through (if ever) and get to the end.

> *Years ago was a radio program, "Bob and Ray." They would put on verbal skits that were beyond funny. I'd be in tears from laughing. They were very serious about their topics and would get in a huge disagreement over some obscure issue.*
>
> *One time they played members of two clubs, "The Slow Talkers of America," and "The Fast Talkers of America." When the Slow Talker would start a point, the Fast Talker would finish it, but the Slow Talker wouldn't stop talking with his point. The Fast Talker would get hysterical to get to the end sooner, interrupt, and finish the conversation - he thought. But the Slow Talker would continue on unperturbed to the agonizing end of his point. Oh, God! It was SO people! I laughed 'til I cried!*

INTRODUCE A NEW IDEA - SPEAK SLO-O-WLY

But, we have to assume that you're giving information because the audience doesn't know something they need to know – doesn't that make sense?

And, if they don't know what they need to know, you need to speak "slow....**ER**" than usual so the audience can assimilate the new information or evidence – make sense? Speak a little slower so the points can be noted.

Usually what happens with new information, people think over the points as the speech rolls along, but sometimes they miss the in-coming information. It might be profitable, on occasion, to repeat the point you made to be sure everyone gets it.

For new information, or to describe a new technique or new discovery; if there's a need to emphasize or to impress, speak SLO-W-**ER**, not ssslllooowww –

When you introduce critical new evidence, a specific piece of information, book title - anything where you need total attention, take a split second to "set up" the audience – alert them to take notice - use a transition.

To "set up" the audience to focus on you, introduce your idea. Suppose you discovered a new will negating the current will. Hold up the new will so it's visible to all, pause (the pause is critical –silence speaks loudly).

TIME…take it – yes, take your time. Not so slow you drive the fast-thinkers nuts, but a, purposeful s-l-o-w - that's a sign of control, deliberation, maturity and comprehension of what you're doing - impressive! In America timing is critical yet we greatly admire anyone in control of his actions.

Watch the audience' reaction; space your movements deliberately and cautiously. Not like the character, Arragon, in "The Merchant of Venice," Portia retorts,

"Too long a pause for that which you find." Shakespeare

LESS IS BETTER. On TV a re-enacted murder trial resulted in a hung jury. The second time around, the Prosecutor eliminated all information except the actual facts affecting the case. He won the case on the assumption, "Don't confuse the jury with too much information". To quote the old TV program, "Dragnet": "Just the facts, Ma'm - just the facts." Sometimes, less is enough.

MEDIATION – "BRICOLAGE" is a French word, meaning, "bits and pieces". Devised by a professor at Columbia this method helps communicate with "opponents" in mediation. You adjust the "language" of your dispute; one side speaks in triangles, the other side speaks in circles.

How does the mediator find a common language between the two sides?

Since communication is imperfect (as we humans tend to be) some triangles are rounded at the corners and some circles have a pointed edge. Match these "bits and pieces" so they create a new language both sides can speak.

For example, what does everyone have in common? Well, the "language" everyone can speak is: A need for security, for one thing.

> A place to rest your head.

> Something to eat when you need it.

> Freedom from fear, a threat of physical danger.

These concepts are fairly universal.

EMPATHY WITH THE OPPOSITION Using bricolage. Put yourself in their place - the other side as well as your side. As far

INTRODUCE A NEW IDEA - SPEAK SLO-O-WLY

as you possibly can, ask yourself, "How do they feel? What do they want? How can I resolve this issue so both sides could win, or my side win with minimal psychological damage to either party?"

The problem here is you don't want to give the impression you're for the opponents, yet if you can avoid rancor, it makes life better for everyone.

FAILURE is an opinion. This is the part where I get to be the crone - my favorite role. I've lived many years longer than most of you who are reading this book, and I can tell you with deepest honesty and pleasure that sometimes when you "fail," it's the best thing that could have happened to you. I have learned when one door shuts, another opens and you step right in. Hold your head up high and walk on.

THE "LITTLE" GUYS In particular, listen to the "little" guys, the custodian, maids, garbage men, coffee servers, mail people. Often I would forget my keys to something and the custodian would always let me in where I needed to go. The hotel maids and cleaning ladies are very smart, get on their good side for extra information. A custodian used to clean up waste paper and give me valuable, useful data someone tossed out.

Especially your support team needs your approval, as much as possible, and your guidance when necessary. Whenever possible say, "Thank you," and with a smile or happy face.

I have an anecdote I think you attorneys will find particularly interesting:

> *As a Communication Studies Instructor I had a student who was a well-known sportscaster. As a speaker he was outstanding, as a student, he was not. As a student he was basically an arrogant, obnoxious jock. The class*

requirements and his submissions bore no resemblance to each other. His attendance was, apparently when he had nothing more pressing to do. He received a "C" for the class grade. Outraged, he went directly to the Dean and the Chair of the Department and ordered them to order me to change his grade. Both the Dean and the Chair were wimps, terrified of jocks. They put a great deal of pressure on me, "only a woman," to change his grade. I refused. Another faculty member was worried about me and said, Carolyn, if you don't change his grade, they'll have to bring in the lawyers!" I thought that was hysterically funny! Bring in the lawyers!! Yes! Please! Bring in people who can think!! Much to my disappointment they didn't bring in the big guns and they left his grade at a "C."

My qualifications for this book are years of suing and being sued, 30 years college Instructor of Communication Studies, trained opera singer, seasoned stage performer, and my cousin's a lawyer.

If I haven't addressed a concern of yours, please let me know how I can help you.

Thank you, for being there when we're backed into a legal corner – you're the one in the white hat and white horse with the William Tell Overture playing in the background! Your words are silver bullets!

For more insight, food for thought, I suggest you read:

    The Prince (Machiavelli)

    Meditations (Marcus Aurelius)

    The Devil and Daniel Webster (Stephen Vincent Benet)

INTRODUCE A NEW IDEA - SPEAK SLO-O-WLY

Merchant of Venice (W. Shakespeare)

"If" for Boys (Rudyard Kipling)

The Screwtape Letters (C.S. Lewis)

ABOUT THE AUTHOR

Carolyn Franklin

M. A. Communication Studies

M. A. Education

B. A. Psychology

30 years voice training (San Francisco Opera)

Voice/Speech improvement Coach

voicedynamicscf@yahoo.com

OTHER BOOK BY CAROLYN FRANKLIN

Police Brutality: A solution

Adam: First man, or, first mouse?

Emotional Intelligence: Like yourself

Coping With Bullies: A gentle approach

You Can Catch More Flies With Honey: The Art Of Rhetoric, Persuasion, Manipulation, and Blarney

Your Voice – Your Personality The Total You

Women Bullying Women: An effect of Women's Lib

Rx For Your Communication Ills - The ULTIMATE Book on Communication

Women At Work: Win-Win Communication Strategies

#MeToo, NOW, Women's Lib, Just Say No: Why they won't work

Athena: Goddess of Communication Strategies

Welfare + Diversity: Social Suicide

The Story of Mary: Mayhem, mirth and miracles

www.ingramcontent.com/pod-product-compliance
Lightning Source LLC
Chambersburg PA
CBHW070956240526
45469CB00016B/1444